EXTENDED LIFE C.T.M.

SPIRITUAL WARFARE

A Biblical Perspective

Karen E. Connell

Adapted from the book
EVEN THE VERY ELECT Will Be Deceived
By Karen E. Connell

www.extendedlife.net

ISBN-13:978-0615632094

ISBN-10:0615632092

Bible quotes are from several Bible versions. The particular Bible version is indicated by the following abbreviations.

KJV   The King James Version of the Bible. Published by Thomas Nelson Inc.

NKJV   The New King James Version of the Bible.

NIV   The Holy Bible, New International Version. Copyright 1973, 1978, 1984, by the International Bible Society.

NLT   New Living Translation Bible. Copyright THE LOCKMAN FOUNDATION,1960, 1962, 1963, 1968, 1971, 1973, 1975, 1977.

AMP   The Amplified Bible. Copyright by Zondervan Publishing House, 1965, Grand Rapids, Michigan.

Word studies and definitions are from several sources. The particular source is indicated by the following abbreviations.

STR   Biblesoft's New Exhaustive Strong's Numbers and Concordance With Expanded Greek and Hebrew Dictionary. Copyright © 1994 Biblesoft & International Bible Translators, Inc.

THAY   Thayer's Greek Lexicon (Complete and Abridged Formats) Electronic Database. Copyright © 2000 by Biblesoft and International BibleTranslators, Inc.

B/D/B   Brown-Driver &Briggs Hebrew Lexicon, Copyright © 1993Woodside Bible Fellowship, Ontario, Canada, Licensed from the Institute for Creation research

CWSD   The Complete Word Studies Dictionary: AMG Publishers, 2003. Electronic Database Copyright © 1998, 2003 by Biblesoft.

APPRECIATION

I am blessed and thankful for all those who have encouraged me to continue sharing the word of God with all who have ears to hear what the Spirit is saying to His Church in these end times. I am so grateful to my beloved husband Garry, who especially encourages me with his enduring love and his devoted servant's heart. I am also grateful to our co-laborer Martin Roos for his faithfulness and labor of love with the tedious task of proof reading.

DEDICATION

This book is dedicated to all those who are serious about becoming trained and equipped in order to do the work of their ministry.

Table of Contents

AUTHOR'S NOTE

I have been a serious student of God's word for over 40 years. During this time I have studied the King James Version as my preferred version of the Bible. I believe it to be the most reliable translation available. This is the version I also use for Scripture memorization. Since the Bible was not written in English, I make it a point to study Bible texts according to their original meanings as they were written in the Hebrew and Greek. I do however; use a variety of Bible translations in my writing and teaching ministries, in order to emphasize a Scriptural truth I am trying to relate. There is no way one single English translation can convey the depth of God's truth contained in the original Greek and Hebrew word meanings. Readers often miss the full impact of truth found in familiar verses of Scripture because they are used to hearing a verse the same way every time it is read or quoted. I have often thought I understood all there was to know about a certain verse until I heard it rendered in a different way, or checked it out in the original languages. In any case the Holy Spirit is our teacher. I have read certain verses in various translations and heard the Holy Spirit say "looks this up in the original" Hebrew or Greek only to be amazed at how much God had to say!

My intent then, for using various Bible translations is to make clear a truth I am conveying from God's word. For the same reason I do not always quote an entire verse, but focus on the phrase that is making my point. Jesus and the Apostles often quoted only a portion of an Old Testament Scripture to make their point. We must also remember that verse divisions and numbers were not added to Bible translations until around   1560 A.D.

INTRODUCTION

There is much being taught and written on the subject of *spiritual warfare* within many Christian circles. For over forty years I have personally been involved in several Christian movements, namely the Pentecostal, Charismatic and most recently the New Apostolic Reformation (NAR) movement, all of which taught and practiced some form of spiritual warfare. As with many other practices and beliefs that I have been exposed to in these movements, God has been faithful to reveal and make plain to me through His Word, many of the errors and excesses that were occurring. Some of these things I had embraced for a time because I either lacked knowledge of what the word of God said about these things or because I neglected to carefully seek God and weigh what I was seeing and hearing by what His word has to say.

In this booklet I will be sharing some the insights and revelations the Lord has graciously given to me in order to keep me from following some of the popular beliefs and practices related to spiritual warfare that are contrary to the Scriptures. Since falling prey to many deceptions in my early life as a Christian, which could have had devastating *eternal consequences* for me, I have been strongly determined to seek the Lord regarding any teachings or practices that I encounter within any movement among professing Christians. I know from my own painful experiences how subtle Satan's deception can be and how easily a professing Christian can be swayed by his deceptive methods and strategies. I have learned to weigh everything according to the only true and accepted standard of God, namely His Holy and inspired Word—the Bible!

Far too many sincere Christians are falling prey to being mesmerized by flamboyant and spiritual looking ministers and ministries that are leading them down the garden path of deception, when it comes to the subject of spiritual warfare. Why is this? Mainly because there is a prideful quest for *power—control—recognition* which is being legitimized through false teachers and teachings, some of which will be elaborated on in this study. For more on this subject you can read my book *NORMALIZING EVIL Through False Teaching.* The motivating force behind all of this is Satan's anti-Christ spirit. His motivations and agendas are producing his ungodly characteristics within professing Christians that have been duped by false teachers and practices concerning spiritual warfare.

I pray that you will seriously consider what is written within these pages and heed the warning that the Apostle Paul gave to sincere followers of Jesus Christ...

> *I know full well that false teachers , like vicious wolves, will come in among you after I leave, not sparing the flock... Even some of you will distort the truth <u>in order to draw a following</u> (Acts 20:29-30, NLT).*

Chapter 1

Spiritual Realms of Delegated Authority

"For we do not wrestle against flesh and blood, but against principalities, against powers, against the rulers of the darkness of this world, but against spiritual wickedness in the heavenly places" (Ephesians 6:12, KJV).

Listed below is a breakdown of *key words* from the above very familiar verse that is foundational to the subject of spiritual warfare. This text reveals Satan's *spiritual hierarchy.* Understanding this hierarchy is important because it reveals that our fight is not against people! People can be a problem or have problems and certainly create serious problems, but our warfare is against what Satan uses to manipulate and control **people**. What He uses are:

- **Principalities**… (Strong's 746, Gr. *arche*) literally means *the first or head ruler in a place of power, dominion and authority.* Satan's *head rulers* are

8

depicted as ten *"horns"* in (Revelation 17:12) and as the *"Prince of Persia"* and *"Greece"* in (Daniel 10:13 and 20). These "spiritual principalities" are head rulers over nations. They fought against Michael who is the spiritual principality (head ruler) assigned to the nation of Israel.

- **Powers...** (Strong's 1849, Gr. *exousia*) means "delegated authority." Satan, his angels and demons all have <u>delegated authority by God</u>—to use their deceptive influence within countries, geographic, economic and political regions, cities, neighborhoods, organizations (including churches) and individuals. Even though their influence is evil, God who is sovereign over all, uses these evil beings to accomplish His purposes *"...For there is no authority* (exousia) *except from God, and the authorities* (exousia) *that exist are appointed by God" (Romans 13:1, NKJV, parenthesis mine).*

- **Rulers** ... (Strong's 288, Gr. *kosmokrator*) t h e s e are "world rulers." Satan and his angels are appointed a place for ruling in the world from lawfully appointed thrones of iniquity through which their "evil" is "devised" ... *"Shall the <u>throne of iniquity</u>, which <u>devises evil by</u>* (God's) *<u>law</u>, have fellowship with You? (Psalm 94:20, NKJV, parenthesis mine).*

In (Psalm 94:20) we are given insight into the fact that all principalities and rulers operate not only by God's "power" (exousia) but also according to His **law** (Strong's 2706). The word "law" literally means that God (who is the head over all principalities and rulers) has *rightfully appointed a deserved time* for a **throne of iniquity** to **devise evil** (Strong's 3335 & 5999).

The literal meanings to these words portray bringing *immense pressure to bear upon the minds and bodies of individuals, that results in pain—worry and trouble of all kind.* This evil "pressure" is brought to bear upon the **iniquity** (sinful tendencies) of unrepentant people, as God's judgment upon their sin. This is what Job went through in order for God to reveal to him the power if his pride.

When a throne of iniquity is established it is because sin has given the devil the right to operate... *Neither give place to the devil (Ephesians 4:27, KJV).* The word *place* is the Greek word (Strong's 5117) *topos* (top'os), which means *the right, license or condition.* Sin is the *condition* that gives the devil the *right* or the *license* to establish a throne of *iniquity.*

However, in (vs.21) we are told that if a person is *righteous* (their sin is repented of and under the blood of Jesus) the devil does not have the *right* to rule over them from a throne of iniquity...

> *They* (evil beings) *gather together against the life of the righteous, And condemn innocent blood. But the LORD is my defense, And my God the rock of my refuge (Psalm 94:21-22, NKJV).*

In (vs. 23) we are told that when evil powers try to overstep their delegated authority, <u>God will</u> step in (not us) and deal with them...

> *He has brought on them their own iniquity, And shall cut them off in their own wickedness; The LORD our <u>God shall cut them off</u> (Psalm 94:23, NKJV).*

The *principalities, powers and rulers of darkness* dwell in the "heavenly places.

- **Heavenly Places** ... (Strong's 2032, Gr. *epouranios*) means "a place in the realm of the spirit." Thrones are seats or sources of power that are established in <u>heavenly places</u>. God has

His "heavenly place" as do the principalities, powers and rulers of the kingdom of darkness. There are three realms that spiritual beings are given delegated authority to operate in.

Three Spiritual Realms

There are "three" spiritual realms that need to be clearly understood because each realm is a sphere of authority designated by God.

The first spiritual realm ...is found within *individuals.* It is the realm of the *human spirit* from where spiritual life or death influences and affects a person's soul and body. It is where Satan establishes his kingdom of darkness and spiritual death. It is also the realm where God establishes His Kingdom of life through righteousness, peace and joy when we are persuaded to believe and respond to the Gospel of Jesus Christ. When a human's spirit is in darkness Satan has access to the life of that individual—like he did with Judas Iscariot... *And having dipped the bread, He gave it to Judas Iscariot, the son of Simon... Now after the piece of bread, Satan entered him (John13:27, NKJV).*

The battle for the souls (minds) of people begins by doing battle for their hearts (spirits) where the powers of darkness rule within individuals who have no spiritual life or light. ...*having their understanding darkened, being alienated from the life of God, because of the ignorance that is in them, because of the blindness of their heart...who, being past feeling, have given themselves over to.. work all that is unclean* (demonic) ... *(Ephesians 4:18-19, NKJV).* God has given us His delegated authority to do battle for the hearts of men so they can be

11

delivered from the powers of darkness and be translated into God's kingdom… ***Who has delivered us from the power of darkness, and has translated us into the kingdom of his dear Son (Col 1:13, KJV).*** This is the only realm where we have delegated authority to do spiritual warfare. We are called to establish the kingdom of God in this realm—within the spirit of individuals. ***"…behold, the kingdom of God is <u>within you</u> (Luke 17:21, KJV).***

<u>The second spiritual realm</u> …is in the air or *atmosphere* over the earth. This is the realm where spirits exist (God's and Satan's) and these spirits (good and bad) exert their power (delegated authority) over individuals and *people groups* according to the "law" decreed or appointed by God. <u>This is a spiritual dimension or realm that humans are not given God's delegated authority to operate in.</u> This is the realm where spirit beings have *exclusive power* and authority (exousia). This point will be elaborated on later in this study. The greater the number of individuals who are ruled by sin the greater influence Satan has over the world through this realm where spirit beings have delegated power. From this realm people groups on earth are influenced by spiritual forces. From here Satan can accomplish his spiritual wickedness through his "<u>high place</u>" (the atmosphere or second heaven) that can affect *sinners* in corporate settings such as nations, cities, religious groups, families, institutions and businesses. "…***the <u>prince of the power of air</u>,*** (is a ruler who has delegated authority in the atmosphere) ***the spirit that now <u>works in the children of disobedience</u>*** (on the earth) … *(Ephesians 2:2, KJV).*

<u>The third spiritual realm</u> …is the "third" heaven. The Apostle Paul mentions being caught up to the "third heaven" where God's throne is located (2 Corinthians 12:2). This is the place of God's power (delegated authority). God has exclusive power in this spiritual realm. This is where all saved believers will be seated

12

with Christ in the ages to come, in a place of ultimate honor and authority.

> *"...by grace you have been saved, and* (He) *raised us up together, and made us sit together <u>in the heavenly places in</u>* (literally: in heaven with) *Christ Jesus...* (so) *that <u>in the ages to come</u> He might show the exceeding riches of His grace in His kindness toward us* (who are) *in Christ Jesus (Ephesians 2:5-7, NKJV).*

This text is one of the most misused by many who teach things concerning our spiritual authority when it comes to *strategic level spiritual warfare* (a term invented by C. Peter Wagner). He invented this term to identify the different "levels" that spirits operate in. More will be said about this in a later chapter of this study. However, God's third "heaven" is a literal place that contains a city called the "New Jerusalem" that is going to be transferred from the third heaven to "New Earth" at the end of the ages...

> *And I John saw the holy city, new Jerusalem, <u>coming down from God out of heaven</u>, prepared as a bride adorned for her husband (Revelation 21:2, KJV).*

Meanwhile, Satan is mentioned as *visiting* a place, presumably before God's throne (because it is a place of accountability) in the third heaven. I say *visiting* because he was cast out of heaven when he sinned and took one third of the angels with him in his rebellion and they no longer live there. The Bible gives the following account of the time when Satan *visited God's heaven* with other "sons of God" (angels) who were evidently summoned to give an account of what they had been doing ...

> *Now there was a day when the sons of God came to present themselves before*

> *the LORD, and Satan also came among*
> *them... And the LORD said to Satan,*
> *"From where do you come?" So Satan*
> *answered the LORD and said, "From*
> *going to and fro on the earth, and from*
> *walking back and forth on it"*
> *(Job 1:6-7, NKJV).*

These then are the "three spiritual realms" mentioned in the Bible. Because many professing Christians lack a Biblical understanding of the "exousia" (delegated authority) for each realm, those who are ignorant concerning these three realms, are intruding into this forbidden "second realm of the spirit" (the second heaven).

> *Let no one cheat you of your reward,* (by)
> *taking delight in the... worship of angels,*
> *intruding into those things which he has*
> *not seen, vainly puffed up by his fleshly*
> *mind (Colossians 2:18, NKJV).*

This text clearly talks about people who insist on looking into *or* "intruding into" the "realm" of angels, because of their *spiritual pride.* As previously stated this is a realm they should not be looking or prying into, because it is an occult realm of deception (hidden from humans) where information *can be obtained* from spiritual beings (as evidenced by many modern day physics).[1] The term *worship of angels* is used in this verse also. The word *worship* is the Greek word (Strong's 2356) *threskeia* (thrace-ki'-ah) which according to the CWSD... *alludes to the false, gnostic doctrine of spiritual exaltation in which human worshipers were permitted to share in the ... activities of various grades of angelic beings.* People who seek "spiritual experiences" often intrude into the realm and activities of *spiritual beings* from

---

[1] The word *not* as used in the phrase *which he has not seen* in (Col 2:18) is not included in the traditional original Alexandrian text, but was added in the 27th edition of the Nestle-Aland Greek New Testament and the United Bible Societies 4th edition. Either way it implies that we are not to be intruding into this spirit realm by *seeing* things in this realm which do exist.

different levels of Satan's hierarchy. This only results in a false *spiritual exaltation* (spiritual pride) and their spiritual demise.

This false super spiritualism is a work of the devil. This is why Jesus said He needs to be made known in the earth. His purpose is to destroy Satan's ability to influence and deceive people. ***"For this purpose the Son of God was manifested, that <u>he might destroy the works of the devil</u>" (1 John 3:8, KJV).***

Jesus said in (John 14:12) that the works He did we would do also. The works of Jesus included dealing with spirits and their deceptive works. Jesus made it very plain when the devil was at work in the lives of the "super-spiritual" religious leaders of His day. Therefore, we must not ignore demonic activity when we realize it is at "work" but acknowledge and embrace the mission Jesus gave to us.

> ***"The Spirit of the Lord is upon me, because he hath anointed me to preach the gospel to the poor; he hath sent me to heal the brokenhearted, to preach deliverance to the captives, and recovering of sight to the blind, to set at liberty them that are bruised" (Luke 4:18, KJV).***

Jesus has delegated his authority to destroy the "works" of the devil <u>within the lives of people</u>, and this has been given to every one of His true followers. Therefore, if we are indeed true followers, we have the "lawful right" to do spiritual warfare the way Jesus and the Apostles did spiritual warfare so salvation can be embraced by the lost and the deceived within our churches. In order to accomplish this task, Jesus gave us supernatural "dunamis" can do power (Strong's 1411) and supernatural "weapons" for spiritual warfare which include His "Spiritual gifts" and His Word.

> ***"We do not war according to the flesh...***
> ***For the weapons of our warfare are not***

15

> *carnal but mighty in God for pulling down strongholds" (2 Corinthians 10:3-4 NKJV).*

Bringing salvation means releasing people from sin and demonic activity in their lives and this requires the use of God's supernatural gifts if we are to accomplish the greater works that Jesus said we are to do (for a comprehensive study on the subject of spiritual gifts I recommend my *Spiritual Gifts Manual*). "How shall we (or they) escape if we neglect so great a salvation?

> *After it was at the first spoken through the Lord, it was confirmed to us by those who heard, God also bearing witness with them, both by signs and wonders and by various miracles <u>and by gifts of the Holy Spirit</u> according to His own will" (Hebrews 2:2-4, NAS, parenthesis mine).*

Spiritual gifts must accompany the Word of God in order to be effective as "defensive and offensive weapons" that will destroy the works of darkness within people. Jesus, who is the Word of God, died to give these gifts to His followers.

> *"In conclusion, be strong in the Lord, be empowered through your union with Him; draw your strength from Him, that strength which His boundless might. Put on God's whole armor...the armor of a heavy-armed soldier which God supplies, that you may be able to successfully stand up against all of the strategies and the deceits of the devil"(Ephesians 6:10-11, AMP).*

Chapter 2

False Spiritual Warfare

"...wage a good warfare, (by) having faith and a good conscience..." (1 Timothy 1:18-19, NKJV).

According to Scripture, it is God's will to destroy the power and works of the devil by the spiritual warfare of His saints. Please notice that it is the *"power and works"* of the devil that we are to destroy - not "the devil" or "angels" and "demons." The devil and his followers will be destroyed at the end of the ages <u>by God Himself</u>. Many well intentioned Christians try to get rid of demons or principalities by cursing, binding or removing them from a "territory" or "nation" to which they are assigned. But these Christians are deceived! According to the Bible, spirit beings have been given a place of delegated authority by God to dwell in the <u>*second heaven*</u>, as we have already discussed. If they leave that delegated place they are breaking the law established by God. All lawlessness is punished by God.

> *And I remind you of the angels who did* *not stay within the limits of authority God gave them but <u>left the place where they belonged</u>. God has kept them chained in prisons of darkness, waiting for the Day of Judgment (Jude 6, NLT).*

Angels who have been assigned to the second heaven who fail to obey God's law regarding their <u>*assigned place of authority*</u> are punished. They cannot leave their delegated place of authority and we have no authority to make them leave. The only time spirit beings (known as demons) are removed from their abiding place is when they are cast out of "people." Even then they can return to re-occupy those who do not fill that abiding place with God's Holy Spirit. As long as sin is practiced in a territory, nation or in an individual's life, demonic powers have lawful "authority" which is the legal right to do the works of the devil in that place.

Humans will always fall prey to *spiritual pride* when they intrude into the forbidden realm of spiritual beings. Our fallen human natures love the *recognition* it receives when we are perceived (by ourselves or others) as being *super spiritual* because we can intrude into this forbidden realm. I want to make it perfectly clear that true believers do receive *spiritual revelation,* but only because God chooses to reveal His truth to our born again spirit of light *<u>through His word</u>.*

Christians are being deceived into thinking that information they may receive regarding *spirits* and their *activities* is a *spiritual revelation* given to them by God. However God does not violate His own word! What pertains to this forbidden realm of the spirit is *kept hidden from us* by God Himself—for our own protection. If we insist on intruding into this realm and in being involved in false *spiritual worship* we are in grave danger of God's burning anger...

> **They turned to serve and <u>worship</u> other gods** (spirit beings) **that were foreign to them, gods** (spirit beings) **that the LORD had <u>not designated for them</u>... That is why the LORD's anger burned ... bringing down all the curses recorded in this book. ..."<u>There are secret things that belong to the LORD our God</u>, but the revealed things** (from His word) **belong to us and our descendants forever, so that we may obey His words... (Deuteronomy 29:26-27, 29,** *Parenthesis mine).*

False teaching concerning spiritual warfare is actually encouraging occult practices and is not only leading God's people astray but right into the Lake of Fire! False spiritual warfare teachers are telling their followers they need to do things like *spiritual mapping* and seek revelation and information about what spirits are in certain geographical areas such as where *mountains* (high places) and *portals* (openings into the forbidden spirit realm) exist. Many are intruding into this realm in order to find out this information about spiritual beings. They erroneously believe by doing so they can effectively do spiritual warfare against evil spiritual beings by binding their power over people, cities and nations. Instead, all they are doing is entering into a forbidden "occult" realm and are becoming thoroughly deceived! God forbids His people from operating in this "spiritual realm", which is called the realm of "sorcery" (a place of forbidden and hidden knowledge). This is the place where *familiar spirits*, *seducing spirits*, and *lying spirits* dwell, which have the ability to <u>charm</u>, <u>enchant</u> and <u>bewitch</u> those who enter this realm...

> **"There shall not be found among you any one that makes his son or his daughter to**

pass through the fire, or that uses divination, or is an observer of times, or an enchanter, or a witch, or a charmer, or a consulter with familiar spirits, or a wizard, or a necromancer (in order to receive communication or revelation). *For all that do these things are an abomination to the Lord: and because of these* (being) *abominations* (to) *the Lord your God... drive them out from before you. You shall be perfect with the Lord your God."* *(Deuteronomy 18:10-13, KJV, parenthesis mine).*

The desire for the power to control what happens in the spirit realm has actually led deceived Christians into doing dangerous things like studying occult resources such as the Satanic Bible, the mystical Jewish writings of the Kabala, as well as many other sources of pagan material, in order to obtain secret spiritual knowledge used by Satan so they can receive revelation into how their enemy operates. Those who do such things are deceived into believing that whatever *knowledge* they may be receiving is coming from God's Holy Spirit, but in truth it is coming from Satan's unholy spirits. There are numbers of well-known Christian leaders who promote unscriptural practices like spiritual mapping (already mentioned), and ascribing *prophetic significance* to various "signs" and even practices such as *setting occult ley lines!*

Pulling Down Strongholds

It is not only alarming to see so many deceived professing Christians getting involved in "spiritual warfare" practices that are forbidden; but it is just as devastating to see their focus is no longer on transforming the realm of the *inner man* (the human spirit is our only realm of delegated power). Instead the focus has been diverted to *transforming the world* through the use of *unlawful power and practices*. If Satan can fool us into thinking that our false spiritual warfare antics can—map out, march out, decree out or pray out spirits from their delegated realm of authority, he can keep us busy spinning our wheels! Dr. Orrel Steinkamp, puts it this way...

> Pragmatically speaking, one of the dangers of *strategic level spiritual* warfare [a term invented by C. Peter Wagner] is that it will deplete the energies of Christians. After all the prayer walks, marches, prayer expeditions and driving *ad nauseam,* the Christian community will hardly have the energy to slog it out in preaching and teaching the Gospel, which Paul said was *"the power of God unto salvation"* (Romans 1:19) and which (Hebrews 12:4) states is *"sharper than any two edged sword."* [2] (Brackets mine).

Not to mention all these man made spiritual warfare techniques can become seemingly complicated and extremely time consuming and exhausting—as I can attest from my own involvement in such things! Nowhere in Scripture are we taught that our calling is to transform the world by warring against Satan's hierarchy. Many assume this is the case because of what the Bible states in (Ephesians 6:12), but a closer look at what this verse is literally saying (which I will discuss in another part of this study), reveals this is not the case. We are simply given the revelation from God that this hierarchy does exit. But we are told our high calling is to transform people by persuading them to change their minds about SIN and their need for Jesus Christ as their Savior.

As I discussed we are warned about being cheated out of the *reward* (forgiveness—eternal life) of our *high calling*

---

[2] Dr. Orrel Steinkamp, "The Technology Of Spiritual Warfare Evangelism," The Plumbline, Vol. 7, N0 1.
http://www.deceptioninthechurch.com/orrel9.html

(Colossians 2:18), which Satan is subtly doing through false teachings like those concerning spiritual warfare. One way this is happening is that the basic sinful nature of man is no longer the issue being preached by a lot of Christian leaders; instead the issue is manifesting power and dominion over the enemy, and obtaining positions of power and recognition here on earth. Those in this place believe spiritual enemies need to be continually bound, cast down and overthrown and warred against, otherwise they will continue to break down our cities, steal our children and destroy our nations! Jesus said _He came to destroy the works of the enemy_, (not us) which means if we preach Jesus the enemy's <u>works</u> will be destroyed! Multitudes have lost the *simplicity* of preaching Jesus Christ.

> **But I fear, lest somehow, as the serpent deceived Eve by his craftiness, so your minds may be corrupted from the <u>simplicity that is in Christ</u>... For if he who comes preaches another Jesus whom we have not preached, or if you receive a different spirit which you have not received, or a different gospel which you have not accepted — you may well put up with it! (2 Corinthians 11:3-4, NKJV).**

It is NOT the spiritual forces in the spirit realm that need to be pulled down. But it is what people think and what they believe which are the *strongholds* that need to be pulled down and made subject to Jesus Christ.

> **For the weapons of our warfare are not carnal, but mighty through God to the <u>pulling down of strong holds</u>... Casting down <u>imaginations</u>, and every high thing that exalteth itself against the knowledge of God, and bringing into captivity every thought to the obedience of Christ (2 Corinthians 10:4-5, KJV).**

Scripture does not teach that we are to "pull down" principalities or demonic rulers and cast them out of a nation or city in order to pull down Satan's strongholds. We are told, however, to pull down the "strongholds" they have built, which again are false imaginations (erected by lies and doubts). Study the context of the only verse in Scripture that tells us about *strongholds* and you find that it speaks about "imaginations" (this subject is discussed in great detail in Chapter 2 of my book *EVEN THE VERY ELECT Will Be Deceived*).

We have no <u>power</u> (exousia-delegated authority from God) to destroy demons or to even "bind them" as I will soon discuss. In other words, we are not empowered to fight and destroy demons themselves. But we are empowered to fight against their "works" which include their "strategies and deceits" that give them the power to do Satan's work in people's lives. There is only one time in Scripture that binding the devil is mentioned, but even this binding is temporary.

> *"I saw an angel coming down from heaven, having the key to the bottomless pit and a great chain in his hand. He laid hold of the dragon, that serpent of old, who is the Devil and Satan, and bound him for a thousand years and he cast him into the bottomless pit, and shut him up, and set a seal on him, so that he should deceive the nations no more till the thousand years were finished. But after these things he must be released for a little while" (Revelation 20:1-3, NKJV).*

The Power To Bind and Loose

There is much false teaching that leads to practicing false spiritual warfare that needs to be addressed. As mentioned these false teachings and ideas are very dangerous because anytime we attempt to operate in a realm of "spiritual power" that is not according to Scripture; we enter into the forbidden realm of "sorcery." This realm is a source of <u>grave deception</u> that can affect sincere Christians. One aspect of false spiritual warfare we must explore is the idea of **"binding and loosing."** Bob Dewaay, in his "Critical Issues Commentary," does a good job of exposing some of the errors connected to this subject. What follows are some excerpts from his articles about binding and loosing.

> "I bind you, Satan!" is uttered in thousands of prayers every day in America. Many books have been written based on the idea that Christians can verbally "bind Satan" and thus "loose" people from his nefarious activities. But in the process, the true Biblical doctrine of binding and loosing is obscured. It might surprise many to find out that **"binding and loosing" are about declaring the terms of** entrance **into the kingdom,** and about determining what is or is not binding on Christians after they have been added to the church. (emphasis mine)[3]

As DeWaay puts it, there are those who believe and practice "binding and loosing" as if it was **"verbal warfare"** against the powers of darkness. One of the key verses used by those who do this kind of spiritual warfare says, *"I will give you the keys of the kingdom of heaven; and whatever you bind on earth shall have been bound in heaven, and whatever you loose on earth shall have been loosed in heaven"* (Matthew 16:19, NASB). DeWaay goes on to explain in his article why this and other verses are not used correctly according to what Jesus said.

> "By combining the thought in (Matthew 16:19) with the (Matthew 12) passage, which speaks of binding the "strong man," they *(false teachers)* draw the conclusion that we have the authority to bind Satan,

---

[3] DeWaay, Robert, *"Binding and Loosing part 1,"* Critical Commentary, pg. 1, www.cicministry.org/commentary

thus making his "goods" exposed for plundering. According to many followers of this theory, the "goods" are money, political power, people, etc. The church supposedly, therefore, has the opportunity to take world power away from Satan and deliver it to ourselves. *(Parenthesis mine)*

What did Jesus mean by the terms "bind" and "loose" as used in (Matthew 16:19)? These words were commonly used by Jewish rabbis. New Testament scholars agree that "binding and loosing," when used in this way, retain the basic meaning that they had in the Jewish culture of the first century. The Theological Dictionary of The New Testament states under the entries for *"deo"* and *"luo"* which are the Greek words for binding and loosing used in (Matthew 16:19) and elsewhere. The customary meaning of the Rabbinic expressions is equally incontestable, namely, to declare (something to be) **forbidden** or **permitted**. DeWaay tells us that A.T. Robertson also comments on the use of the future perfect tense as important.

> If we were to translate the passage very literally, it would read "...whatever you loose on earth shall having been loosed in heaven." The 1995 update version of the NASB (cited above) reflects this tense which the earlier version of the NASB did not. The tense of the verbs shows that the disciples were not unilaterally to decide a matter, thus binding "heaven" to their decision. It means that their decision, as Dr. Robertson suggests, will be in line with what already was God's mind on the issue. This means that the apostles were Jesus' authoritative spokesmen and that **their decisions** (from Jesus) **would be binding**. Jesus spoke God's authoritative words and authorized His apostles to speak those words to the church. We can see this idea in the book of Hebrews:

After it was at the first spoken through the Lord, it was confirmed to us by those who heard, God also bearing witness with them, both by signs and wonders and by various miracles and by gifts of the Holy Spirit according to His own will (Hebrews 2:2-4, NASB).[4]

DeWaay tells us that salvation (being saved or rescued from the works of the devil) or "deliverance" comes by what Jesus has already spoken or taught. It is confirmed by those who **hear from Him** and **speak for Him** when God "bears witness" to the true word of the Lord. The phrase "bear witness" is the Greek word *"sunepimartureo."* It literally means "with superimposed evidence as proof" (Strong's 3140).

Thus the word spoken or taught by the Lord about salvation or deliverance from the power and works of Satan will be proven by true signs, wonders, miracles and gifts. In other words, when we preach the true gospel of salvation, and teach deliverance the way Jesus taught it, we will be given the "weapons of our warfare" (spiritual gifts and the rhema word) to set captives free. Our warfare will then be true and not false warfare.

What DeWaay says must be understood clearly. He tells us that the words "binding and loosing" are usually taken, taught and used **out of context**.

> "Did the apostles ever utter "I bind you, Satan?" Not once is such an utterance recorded in the New Testament. It is not credible to assume that they understood Jesus' teaching as an instruction to "bind Satan" through prayers and verbal declarations and then never followed the instructions personally. The church of the twentieth century should not understand and practice the teachings of Jesus differently than the

---

[4] Ibid, pg. 2. emphasis mine

church of the 1st century. If it does, the authority of Scripture is compromised.[5]

To bind and loose then, is to "forbid" and "permit" something. Therefore the keys to the kingdom of heaven are to permit or forbid what God has already permitted or forbidden in heaven. The "kingdom of heaven" is where the Lord our God dwells on His throne and there is where His decisions are made and carried out by those who are given access to His face, which means those who see things His way.

> *"But the Lord is in his holy Temple; the Lord still rules from heaven. He watches everything closely, examining everyone on earth. For the Lord is righteous, and he loves justice. Those who do what is right will see his face"* **(Psalm 11:4,7, NLT).** *"The Lord has made the heavens his throne; from there he rules over everything"* **(Psalm 103:19, NLT).**

Please notice the context for binding and loosing in the verse below. Peter had a revelation given to him about who Jesus was from the Father "in heaven." The "rock" is Jesus the Christ, the Word of God, and through His Holy Spirit He is the revealer of all truth.

> *Therefore everyone who hears these words of mine and puts them into practice is like a wise man who built his house on the rock. The rain came, the streams rose, and the winds blew and beat against that house; yet it did not fall, because it had its foundation on the rock"* **(Matthew 7:24-25, NIV).**

Peter received this very revelation of the foundation upon which

---

[5] Ibid, pg. 2.

Jesus would build His church from God. *"He said to them,*

> *'But who do you say that I am?' Simon Peter answered and said, 'You are the Christ, the Son of the living God.' Jesus answered and said to him, 'Blessed are you, Simon Bar-Jonah, for flesh and blood has not revealed this to you, but My Father who is in heaven. And I also say to you that you are Peter, and on this rock I will build My church, and the gates of Hades shall not prevail against it. And I will give you the keys of the kingdom of heaven, and whatever you bind on earth will be bound in heaven, and whatever you loose on earth will be loosed in heaven' (Matthew 16:15-19, NKJV).*

The revelation of Jesus Christ as the ROCK, who we are built upon, will not allow the "gates" of hell to prevail against us, the true church. The Greek word for "gate" in this verse is "pule" and it means "entrance" (Strong's 4439). Jesus said that when we have Him as our foundation, "hell," meaning "death," cannot enter into our lives! The Hebrew word for "gate" is even more revealing. It refers not only to "an opening" or "entrance" but also to "thinking" or "reasoning" in its root form (CWSD 8179). In other words, thoughts that come from hell can separate us from God because the word "death" refers to spiritual separation.

Jesus gave us the keys to bind or forbid or to loose or permit **what enters the earth** from the gates or mind of hell. We are people but we are made from the dust of the earth. Therefore, we have a fallen human nature that is "earthly" which can separate us from God if we follow it.

> *"He made peace with everything in heaven and on earth by means of his blood on the cross. This includes you who*

were once so far away from God.
You were his enemies, separated from him
by your evil thoughts and actions"
(Colossians 1:20-21, NLT).

Jesus said His disciples were given the "keys to the kingdom of heaven." What does this mean? First of all, keys lock to "forbid" entrance. Keys also unlock to "permit" entrance of what comes through a door or gate. Keys, therefore, refer to forbidding or permitting "mindsets" from hell that brings death. <u>Mindsets</u> (strongholds) <u>are again demonic works in the form of deceptive thoughts that become effective strategies to separate people from God</u>. Keys represent the authority given to the church "to bind or forbid demonic deceptions and doctrines" from entering the minds of God's people. Keys also represent the Word which brings revelatory light. ***"The entrance of your words gives light; It gives understanding to the simple" (Psalm 119:130, NKJV).***

This is the first of two biblical applications on binding and loosing which are connected to "keys." Now let's examine the second application.

> ***Verily I say unto you, whatsoever you shall bind on earth shall*** *(already have been)* ***bound in heaven: and whatsoever you shall loose on earth shall*** *(already have been)* ***loosed in heaven. Again I say unto you, That if two of you shall agree on earth as touching anything that they shall ask, it shall*** *(already have been)* ***done for them of my Father which is in heaven. For where two or three are gathered together in my name, there am I in the midst of them" (Matthew18:18-20, KJV,*** *parenthesis mine to emphasize the Greek verb tense).*

29

The <u>context</u> for these verses on "binding and loosing" is essential. In the preceding verses, you will find that the context is dealing with sin that is to be forgiven or retained by the one who is confronted with the truth concerning that sin. In other words, the "binding" (declaring as illegal) and "loosing" (removing from obligation, i.e. forgiving the obligation or sin) is according to how a sinner responds. His response will result in being legally bound or loosed from his sin according to the standard "already established" by the court of heaven and revealed to him by Word of God.

We must understand that the only way to bind principalities and powers are to <u>bind their deceptions</u> in order to release sinners from their sin. This does not happen by simply declaring that principalities and powers are bound! This only happens by preaching the Gospel of salvation and by exposing the lies and deceptions of these demonic powers. The more individuals get free from sin and deception in a nation, city, church or family, the less influence and control they will have over them. This is why it is so important to know the "source" for the enemy's deceptions (this will be elaborated on in the last chapter) and especially how they work through sorcery in the minds and lives of people.

Some teach that we have the ability to bind principalities because of the Scripture that Jesus taught concerning "binding the strongman." <u>False teaching always takes verses out of their context to support a false idea.</u> Many have used (Matthew 12:28-29) to teach that the "strongman" is a ruling principality over a territory, city or nation that needs to be cast out. But Jesus taught us to cast demons out of *people*, **not places**. Please notice that according to the context in the following portion of Scripture that what is being taught by Jesus is concerning a demon possessed <u>person</u>.

> *Then one was brought to Him who was demon-possessed, blind and mute; and He healed him, so that the blind and mute man both spoke and saw. And all the multitudes were amazed and said,*

"Could this be the Son of David?" Now when the Pharisees heard it they said, "This fellow does not cast out demons (from people—not territories) *except by Beelzebub, the ruler of the demons." But Jesus knew their thoughts, and said to them: "Every kingdom divided against itself is brought to desolation, and every city or house divided against itself will not stand. If Satan casts out Satan, he is divided against himself. How then will his kingdom stand? And if I cast out demons by Beelzebub, by whom do your sons cast them out? Therefore they shall be your judges. But if I cast out demons by the Spirit of God, surely the kingdom of God has come upon you. Or how can one enter a strong man's house and plunder his goods, unless he first binds the strong man? And then he will plunder his house. He who is not with Me is against Me, and he who does not gather with Me scatters abroad"* (Matthew 12:22-30, NKJV, *parenthesis mine*).

There is only one application that can be correctly given to this text. The strong man's "house" refers to a person not a territory and the "strong man" refers to a demon in that person. The more people that are being manipulated by demonic influence within places of corporate structures (cities, nations, families, etc.) the more power the ruling principalities assigned to these places will be given. On the other hand, the more people are ruled by the Holy Spirit in a city, nation or family, the godlier these places will be!

Many Bible teachers make assumptions based on an analogy that implies things which are not in the actual text. **There is a difference between using true Bible typology, which**

31

represents <u>a truth gleamed from Scripture</u>, and using analogies that imply what Scripture does not say. In the case of the strongman, many false teachers erroneously liken this being to a territorial spirit that needs to be "bound." Then his "goods," which are usually taught as wealth, political power, people, etc., can then be given to the church for our dominion over the earth. The strong man's "goods," however, is the Greek word **"skeuos."** It means "equipment" or "something provided for a specific purpose" (CWSD, 4632). Thus <u>the strong man's goods are his arsenal of "accusations, lies and doubts" coming from demons</u> and these are what we have been given the authority to overrule.

> *Behold, I give unto you power to <u>tread on serpents</u> and <u>scorpions</u>, and over all the power of the enemy: and nothing shall by any means hurt you. (Luke 10:19, KJV).*

In other words, we must first "bind" (forbid) the demon to operate. Jesus has given His believers the authority and supernatural ability to bind or forbid demons from having the freedom to operate within a human being. Jesus demonstrated this power of **forbidding demons to speak** while He was ministering to those who were under their power. *But Jesus rebuked him* (the spirit)*, saying," Be quiet, and come out of him" (Mark 1:25 NKJV).*

It is only after a person is free from hearing their voices that we can "plunder the demons house (abiding place) and their goods meaning the accusations, lies, and doubts, by **exposing them**. In our prayer counseling ministry, we always "forbid" demons from speaking while we are ministering freedom to those we are counseling and praying with. Otherwise, those being ministered to end up hearing all kinds of accusations, lies and doubts, that keep them in confusion and unable or unwilling to make the needed decisions concerning the truth that is being ministered to them.

We have seen demons leave people with little or no effort in many cases by simply forbidding them to speak to those desiring freedom. Then they can clearly hear the truth from God's word and from the Holy Spirit that needs to be understood and received by them. When this is the case and they become willing to accept the truth they are then able to cast down the exposed vain imaginations and the strongman has lost his stronghold over their mind.

This is why we ask people in our counseling ministry to renounce the lies and doubts that gave a demonic spirit power to operate in their lives. Replacing demonic strongholds (mindsets) with the truth insures that when a demon wants to regain entrance, it finds its previous dwelling place not only cleaned out, but filled with the truth of God's Word and with the Holy Spirit.

Many false beliefs and practices are coming out of false spiritual warfare teachings like those we have just examined. What I find most disturbing is what this creates - the worship of "false authority and false authorities." By this I mean, many ministers claim that Jesus gave us "all authority to manipulate cosmic forces." They say we can "permit" (loose) whatever we call "good" in our lives and "bind" (forbid) whatever we decide is evil. But there are many times when bad things are appointed and allowed by God for His ordained purposes. Therefore, we cannot "bind" bad things as a means to stop them through our false spiritual warfare! We must never forget that we have no power to discern good and evil apart from hearing God's Holy Spirit. To eat from that old tree called "the knowledge of good and evil" only results in death. DeWaay puts it this way.

> "I believe that the...'binding and loosing' doctrine feeds these fleshly motivations. It places man at the center rather than God. It is pagan in that a person's destiny is supposedly determined by his ability, or that of others, to gain sufficient 'spiritual knowledge' to manipulate cosmic forces for his own benefit. Biblical Christianity teaches that one's destiny is determined by the work of God and one's response to the gospel of

Jesus Christ. (False teachers claim that) influencing and manipulating cosmic spiritual rulers supposedly determines the salvation and well-being of those involved. (They teach) the way one is to influence these evil forces is through extra-biblical revelations and new spiritual technologies unknown to Christ and His apostles. The New Testament does not support this approach to spiritual warfare.

Biblical Christianity believes in the one true God, the triune God of the Bible. He rules over the entire universe, including all spiritual beings, good or bad. People who know Him through the second person of the trinity, Jesus Christ, have obtained salvation as a gift from God. Through the cross we are in Christ. To be in Christ involves both legal justification and relationship with God. Principalities and powers do not determine our blessedness, spiritual and physical well-being, or eternal destiny [6] (parenthesis mine).

Again, our spiritual warfare is definitely not against spiritual beings themselves. It is against their "works" of deception. But the warfare of Jesus Christ and **His army of angels** (not us) is to battle against evil principalities in the heavenlies, a truth He revealed when He appeared to Daniel. Jesus told Daniel that Michael came to help Him fight against the heavenly principality of Persia and that upon his return there would be another battle with the heavenly ruler of Greece.[21]

There are world rulers in the spirit realm, but given what Jesus revealed to Daniel, we have no authority to pull them down or to battle against them. We must acknowledge that Jesus is called the "Lord of Sabaoth," (Strong's, 4519) the "ruler of the armies" (James 5:4). When these heavenly principalities wage war against us through people and circumstances, we must call upon the Lord because He alone contends against them.

---

[6] Ibid. Pg. 1.

"But in my distress I cried out to theLORD; yes, I prayed to my God for help. He heard me from his sanctuary; my cry reached his ears...He opened the heavens and came down; dark storm clouds were beneath his feet. Mounted on a mighty angel, he flew, soaring on the wings of the wind. He shrouded himself in darkness, veiling his approach with dense rain clouds. The brilliance of his presence broke through the clouds, raining down hail and burning coals. The LORD thundered from heaven; the Most High gave a mighty shout. He shot his arrows and scattered his enemies; his lightning flashed, and they were greatly confused (Psalm 18:6, 9-14, NLT).

We must cry out to Him in prayer when we are attacked by spiritual forces because **He alone will fight these evil heavenly hosts** in their heavenly realm. This prayer of faith is a part of our spiritual arsenal against their works. Mortal man is no match for Spiritual beings. In other words, no mortal being has any power of his own to withstand them. The only power we have is the authority God has given to us over their supernatural works! [7]

It is the pride in man that wants to usurp a place of authority which we have not been given. In (Psalm18) we are told "how and why" God fights on our behalf.

"They attacked me at a moment when I was weakest, but the LORD upheld me. He led me to a place of safety; he rescued me because he delights in me. The LORD rewarded me for doing right; he compensated me because of my

---

[7] Daniel 10:12-13

innocence. For I have kept the ways of the LORD; I have not turned from my God to follow evil. To the faithful you show yourself faithful; to those with integrity you show integrity. To the pure you show yourself pure, but to the wicked you show yourself hostile. You rescue those who are humble, but you humiliate the proud (Psalm 18:18-21, 25-27, NLT).

It is true that demonic powers can influence and even blind the minds of people. The Biblical way to deal with their influence and interference is to cast them out of people and pray that the Lord will battle on their behalf with the spiritual powers influencing them from the heavenlies. Our obligation in spiritual warfare is to PRAY (intercede) and fast for those who need to be free; and PREACH and TEACH God's Word to them because we are only God's mailmen! We deliver our mail to God through prayer and we deliver God's mail to others through preaching and teaching His word.

"The Lord's servants must not quarrel but must be kind to everyone. They must be able to teach effectively and be patient with difficult people. They should gently teach those who oppose the truth. Perhaps God will change those people's hearts, and they will believe the truth. Then they will come to their senses and escape from the Devil's trap. For they have been held captive by him to do whatever he wants" (2 Timothy 2:24-26, NLT).

There is no "easy way" to do the work of the ministry that every Christian is called to do. Every one of us is called to pray for others and to share the gospel message of forgiveness of sin through repentance and faith in Jesus Christ. Chuck Lowe, in his book "Territorial Spirits and World Evangelization?" makes this comment:

"The traditional priority assigned to preaching and prayer was usurped in the 1960s and 1970s by means and methods such as church growth principles, management techniques, and marketing strategies. The over-emphasis on otherwise useful insights and tools led to a relative neglect of the divinely ordained means for conveying spiritual truth and power." [8]

He also tells about a missionary named James Fraser who ministered in Lisu, in southwest China, from 1909 to 1938. The people of Lisu, who knew the reality of demonic harassment, were bound to worshipping demons that manifested through great fear so that the people had physical illness. Lowe writes concerning this:

"Fraser was left with a deepened sense of the malicious power of the evil one, and a renewed urgency for preaching the deliverance which comes through Christ. Facing interminable, excruciating hours of language study alone in his room, Fraser felt his initial enthusiasm draining, and discouragement seeping in to take its place. Exhaustion and despondency often left him vulnerable. In the fifth year of his ministry depression set in, and with it doubt. Suicidal with despair, Fraser eventually recognized the hand of the evil one at work. Satan employs no new weapon against Fraser and the Lisu. Similar strategies are evident in Scripture, and are recorded in the early Church Fathers. In a day when the study of Scripture and of church history is widely neglected, missionary biography may remind Christians of the devil's ways." [9]

---

[8] Lowe, Chuck, *Territorial Spirits and World Evangelism,* 2000, pg. 130.

[9] Ibid. pg. 134-135

Lowe went on to say that the kind of spiritual warfare Fraser used was the kind employed by Jesus and His Apostles. Their warfare practices consisted of diligent labor, patient endurance, and above all, persistent prayer.

> "The opposition (from those you are trying to minister to) will not be overcome by reasoning or pleading, but by (chiefly) steady, persistent prayer. It is a heartbreaking job, trying to deal with a Lisu possessed by a spirit of fear, but the powers of darkness need to be fought. I am now setting my face like flint: if the work seems to fail, then pray; if services etc. fall flat, then pray still more; if months slip by with little or no results, then pray still more and get others to help you" [10](parenthesis mine).

Lowe also reported what Fraser noticed after he spoke about prayer. "Over the next several years, he had occasion to notice the difference prayer made, observing that when he approached people who had received much prayer, half the work seemed already to be done, by an invisible hand." [11]

Lowe also told how Fraser received a personal word from the Lord while he tried to minister in a hamlet on the border of Burma. He experienced great opposition there that left him feeling very discouraged. Then the Lord spoke to him about his situation while he read what God's Word says about discouragement.

"Do not be afraid or discouraged for the battle is not yours but God's. You will

---

[10] Taylor, Geraldine, *Behind the Ranges,* Lutterworth, publisher,London, 1944., pg. 130.

[11] Lowe, Chuck, *Territorial Spirits and World Evangelism,* 2000, pg. 135.

> *not have to fight this battle. Take up your positions and stand firm and see the deliverance the Lord will give you. Do not be afraid, do not be discouraged"* *(2 Chronicles 20:15-17, NAS).*

Because of this personal "rhema" revelation from the Lord, Fraser felt led to pray for the armies of heaven to come down and fight on his behalf against the principalities and powers that influenced the people in the village. Faith rose up in his heart that led him to know he would experience victory and breakthrough which he did! Then he was so encouraged that he went on to the next village and simply "claimed" that place for Christ and expected the same victory. Instead, to his painful dismay, he was horribly rebuffed by the people and later made this entry in his journal; "The defeat was painful, but profitable: and I shall walk more humbly before the Lord- yes and before Satan too, after this." [12] Fraser's account helps to confirm the truth. We cannot walk in the pride of presumption and just "claim" people or territories for the Lord.

How many times do we hear people make these kinds of prideful and empty claims over loved ones that need salvation? We cannot simply "claim" the souls of people, cities and nations for Christ through prayer, declarations and proclamations. Instead, we must go out and do the work of the ministry! The only "legal claims" we have are what God speaks to us through His Word. Thus the work of the ministry is a work of true faith and this faith comes only by hearing the "rhema" word from God (Romans 10:17). Fraser heard God promise him victory. Through receiving a "rhema" word, he had faith for the victory he received. But he also experienced defeat because of his admitted "presumption" that he could just claim and expect a victory for Christ in the next place of his ministry.

---

[12] Taylor, Geraldine, *Behind the Ranges*, pg. 155.

Even though many things claimed for Christ's glory sound noble, these claims do not guarantee fulfillment or victory and especially over the forces of darkness. In other words, our **declarations and proclamations do not obligate God to respond or determine the way in which He will do His work.** He alone is God. He will surely respond to our prayers of faith but not to our prayers of presumption! We are called to resist the forces of darkness, just as Jesus did, by using the written word that God the Holy Spirit brings to our mind. Then it becomes our powerful weapon of offense.

Praying and declaring the "rhema" word is a spiritual weapon we must have ready at all times for spiritual conflict. Lowe completed his comments about Fraser by saying:

"Let us learn from J.O. Fraser – and from others like him – to stand firm on the promises of God (whispered in our ear), to resist the hosts of darkness, to intercede for one another, to pray in detail for the ministry, and to work hard for the glory of God. As Fraser comments: 'here then we see God's way of success in our work, whatever it may be – a trinity of—prayer, faith and patience.' [13](Parenthesis mine).

[13] Lowe, Chuck, *Territorial Spirits and World Evangelism,* pg.146 and Taylor, Geraldine, *Behind the Ranges,* pg. 128

Chapter 3

Qualified Warriors

*You therefore must endure hardship as a **good soldier** of Jesus Christ... No one engaged in warfare entangles himself with the affairs of this life, that he may please him who enlisted him as a soldier (2 Timothy 2:3-4, NKJV).*

Good soldiers are trained and equipped for combat. This means that as God's warriors we must be fully prepared for battle in order to accomplish the *objective* we have been given. The Apostle Paul, one of the greatest spiritual warriors that ever lived, clearly stated the objective of every "good soldier of Jesus Christ...

> *...that I may open my mouth boldly to make known the mystery of the gospel... that in it **I may speak boldly, as I ought to speak** (Ephesians 6:19-20, NKJV).*

41

Unfortunately this objective is being set aside for unscriptural forms of spiritual warfare that have nothing to do with trying to persuade sinners to repent and turn to Jesus as their Lord and Savior. True spiritual warfare requires that we face difficult confrontations for which we must be prepared to handle.

> *... For we wrestle not against flesh and blood, but against principalities, against powers, against the rulers of the darkness of this world, against spiritual wickedness in high (heavenly) places (Ephesians 6:12, KJV).*

The above text is one the most misunderstood and misused verses regarding the true objective for spiritual warfare. This verse in (Eph 6:12) is used by false spiritual warfare teachers to say that we must do battle with spiritual entities called *principalities, powers* and *rulers* of darkness. A closer look at this verse will reveal this is a false premise for true spiritual warfare. Because it is important to understand what God is really saying here, I want to break it down in bite size pieces so this text can be more clearly understood.

First of all in this verse we are told not to *wrestle* with *flesh and blood* (meaning of course other human beings), but our *wrestling* is *against* spiritual beings and their *power* (delegated authority). On the surface this may sound like we are to do battle with spirit beings and their delegated authority. However a closer look at two "key words" in this verse is essential for a true understanding of what God is really telling us.

The first Key word is ... "*wrestle*"(strong's 3823) which is the Greek word *pale* (pal'-ay). This means to be *combative—to struggle with*. Thus we are not to *struggle with* or be *combative with people* (flesh and blood)—which means to fight, argue or become aggressive towards them.

The second Key word is ... "*against*" (Strong's 4314) which is the Greek preposition *pros* (pros) that denotes *motion or* *direction* and according to the CWSD it refers to: *The source from which something proceeds (or continues on)*. Please notice the word *"against"* is used *five times* in this verse.

Translating (Eph 6:12) using these two key words in their literal sense—reveals what God is really telling us ...

> *Don't **wrestle** (aggressively combat) flesh and blood (people) but rather **wrestle** (aggressively be combative) **against** (the source from which **principalities** proceed (continue on)... **against** (the source from which **powers** proceed (continue on) **against** (the source from which rulers of the darkness of this world proceed (continue on) **against** (the source from which **wickedness** in high places proceeds (continue on).*

We are not told to *aggressively combat* the *principalities, powers*, or *rulers,* themselves—but we are told to *aggressively combat* the *source* that allows them to continue on. The phrase *high places* is (Strong's 2032) is the word ***epouranios*** (ep-oo-ran'-ee-os) which refers to a place in the heavens or in the air (the second heaven or abiding place of these spirit beings). So many have been taught we are to enter into battle with these *principalities, powers*, and *rulers* that rule from the second heaven. Many think they are doing *spiritual warfare* by shouting out their so called apostolic and prophetic *authoritative commands* at these spiritual beings which they see as reaping havoc in their territories. Likewise they think spiritual warfare involves railing against these ruling powers in the heavenlies and commanding them to leave or come down from their assigned ruling places. These things unfortunately are nothing more than an exercise in spiritual pride. Here is what God's word says about such people who think they have the authority to control spiritual beings...

> *...those who follow the corrupt desires of the sinful nature and despise* (delegated) *authority* (are)... *Bold and arrogant, these men are not afraid to*

slander celestial beings... yet even angels, although they are stronger and more powerful, do not bring slanderous accusations against such beings in the presence of the Lord (2 Peter 2:10-11, NIV).

Slander involves *false speaking* and *disrespect* for the position and character of the one being slandered. When people fail to realize that God appoints all that have positions authority (on earth and in heaven) they will become puffed up with pride. Jude said this about those who do not honor the delegated authority God has given to the spiritual principalities and rulers in the heavenlies...

Yet these men speak abusively against whatever they do not understand — *these* (prideful utterances) *are the very things that destroy them (Jude 10, NIV, parenthesis mine).*

Combating the Source

What then is the *source* that we are to aggressively combat which is coming from evil spiritual beings in the heavenlies which allows them to continue on? That source, as I previously mentioned, is what Jesus gave all true disciples *delegated authority* or power over. I touched on this before but would now like to dig a little deeper into this text which explains the *source* that we have *delegated authority* over...

Behold, I give unto you <u>power</u> to <u>tread on serpents</u> and <u>scorpions</u>, and over all the <u>power</u> (dunamis—supernatural abilities) *of the enemy: and nothing shall by any means hurt you... Notwithstanding in this rejoice not, that the <u>spirits are subject</u> unto you; but rather rejoice, because your names are written in heaven (Luke 10:19-20, KJV).*

44

In the above text we find that we are given *power* (exousia-delegated authority) from Jesus to do spiritual warfare through an act called "*treading upon*" (Strong's 3817) which is a derivative of the Greek word *paio* (pah'-yo). According to the CWSD: *it means to strike or smite with reference to using—a rod or a sword.* This is a clear picture of bringing *punishment or correction* (the rod)—by using the Word of God (the two edged sword). This correction was to be used against two SOURCES we have been given delegated authority to *aggressively combat.*

- **The first source is serpents** ...it is the Greek word (Strong's 3789) *ophis* (of'-is) and comes from the root word *ophthalmos* (of-thal-mos') in which the CWSD says it refers to what is *seen in the mind*, with a reference to *subtle deception.* When you study the account of what happened in the Garden of Eden, it is clear that sin first came through the *serpent's lies* that produced deception in the mind of Eve. Demonic lies that form *vain imaginations* in the mind of people is one of the evil SOURCES we must aggressively combat with the word of God. When lies coming from spiritual beings are *exposed* and *corrected* by the Word of God, people can then choose to repent. When this is the case the spirits and rulers of darkness have been *tread upon* and have lost the ability (*dunamis*—supernatural ability) to proceed with their influence in the lives of people.

- **The second source is scorpions** ... this comes from the root Greek word (Strong's 4649) *skeptomai* which means *to peer about as a "skeptic"; through the idea of concealment.* This is a picture of the *doubts* (skeptical views) that we are influenced with by evil spirits—so we have doubts about God and His truth, and become *skeptical* towards those who preach and teach the truth as well. Satan was able to *conceal* the doubts he planted in Eve's mind concerning God and the truth He gave her, by subtly disguising his motives for what he was telling her. Doubts not confronted and exposed will proceed to form vain imaginations in the mind. Doubts must also be *tread upon* by being aggressively combated with the Word of God.

There we have it! **Lies** and **doubts** are the <u>source</u> we are called to aggressively combat. Think about it—by embracing Satan's lies and doubts we fall into sin—sickness—cursing. The opposite of a lie is God's truth and the opposite of doubt is to be fully persuaded—which is faith! Truth and faith find their source only in God...

> *...the Spirit of truth, <u>which proceeds</u> <u>from the Father</u> (source), he shall testify of me (John 15:26, KJV).* [14]

Our warfare is done with the only *offensive weapon* that God's warriors have been issued—the *Sword of the Spirit* also called the Word of God. The rest of our GI (God issued) uniform consists of the *defensive armor* of God that every warrior must put on...

> *Put on the whole armor of God, that ye may be able to stand against the wiles of the devil (Ephesians 6:11, KJV).*

The only *wiles* (methods and strategies) then that Satan can use against us effectively are the *lies* and *doubts* his evil powers are able to get us to embrace. As stated these must be corrected with the truth from God's word. A true warrior must be *brave* enough to open their mouth and skilled enough to handle their weapon with God's wisdom. Therefore, true spiritual warriors must learn how to *rightly divide the word of truth* so they are not misusing their weapon by twisting or taking out of context the Word of God—in order to promote their own agendas and ideas.

The breastplate of righteousness will keep our hearts protected, pure and holy so we don't die in the course of our combat duty. Many of God's people have died on their battlefields because

---

[14] Parenthesis mine.

they could not combat the enemy's lies and doubts due to the defilement from unhealed *wounds, bruises and putrefying sores* in their lives.[15] There is no purity and holiness for God's people if they do not look to Him for their healing and deliverance in all unhealed areas of their being. Without complete healing and deliverance from demonic mindsets, God's people will continue to struggle with insecurity and fear and never qualify to become a warrior for God.

> *My people do not consider... Alas, sinful nation, A people laden with iniquity, A brood of evildoers, Children who are corrupters! They have forsaken the LORD, They have provoked to anger The Holy One of Israel, They have turned away backward... Why should you be stricken again? You will revolt more and more. <u>The whole head is sick</u>, And the whole <u>heart faints</u>... From the sole of the foot even to the head, There is no soundness in it, But wounds and bruises and putrefying sores; They have not been closed or bound up, Or soothed with ointment (Isaiah 1:3-6, NKJV).*

Purity In Warfare

As previously stated, the weapons used for true spiritual warfare are not *carnal* weapons but are spiritual weapons. One weapon that is essential in spiritual warfare is that of *holiness*. Demonic powers prey upon and are empowered by our *carnality* (defiled, weak, human ways). These sins are areas of vulnerability that become strongholds for the enemy to gain control over our lives

---

[15] For a complete study on the subject of dealing with defilement from *rejection—bitterness—pride* issues, see authors *Three Fold Cord Healing and Deliverance Manual,* Published by Extended Life Christian Training Ministry, Inc., 2005 revised edition.

from. Holiness therefore becomes a defensive weapon against the attacks of Satan and his rulers…

> *Keep away from every kind of evil… Now may the <u>God</u> of peace <u>make you holy</u> in every way, and <u>may your whole spirit and soul and body be kept blameless</u> until that day when our Lord Jesus Christ comes again… God, who calls you, is faithful; <u>he will do this</u>* (1 Thessalonians 5:22-24, NLT).

God gave this command to the Israelites when they went to war against their enemies…

> *When the army goes out against your enemies, then <u>keep yourself from every wicked</u>* (carnal) *thing… (Deuteronomy 23:9, NKJV, parenthesis mine).*

We must not be fooled into thinking just because self-proclaimed *apostles* can gather a large crowd to do *spiritual warfare* that they have been appointed by God. God goes through our "camps" and is inspecting the lifestyles, ministries and motives of those in these gatherings to see if they meet His standard of holiness…

> *…therefore <u>your camp shall be holy</u>, that He may see <u>no unclean</u> (carnal) <u>thing</u> among you, and turn away from you (Deuteronomy 23: 14, NKJV).*

This text tells us that our "camp" must be holy. The word *camp* literally means the people that you *gather with*—must be holy. In other words, we must not only be careful who we gather together with to do spiritual warfare with, but we must know their personal lives and ministries well enough to know that they are holy people, who believe and minister what is true. We must gather with "holy" (undefiled—blameless Christians) who are of like mind and like faith, even if this means there are only two or three who qualify by having <u>pure motives and lifestyles</u>... ***For where two or three are gathered together in my name, there am I in the midst of them* (Matt 18:20, KJV.** As God's holy warriors gather together for the hearing of God's word, worship and prayer, God says He will be in their midst bringing deliverance from their enemies...

> *"For **<u>the LORD your God walks in the midst of your camp, to deliver you and give your enemies over to you</u>** (Deuteronomy 23: 14, NKJV).*

I have been in many "gatherings" where thousands have come together looking to be entertained by passionate—but compromising false preachers and teachers. These gatherings pride themselves on engaging in new forms of "worship" which they believe the more "crazy and radical" the worship is the more power can be conjured up to "tear a holes in the heavenlies!" Tell me, where in Scripture are we told to "tear holes in the heavenlies" through loud and crazy worship?

Leaders of these kinds of events are teaching our young people that there is "empowerment through becoming radical and extreme" in their public displays of worship. I recall being at one of these "gatherings" where this kind of "crazy and radical" worship was taking place. In this particular youth conference, the worshippers were running to the front of the stage, and "slam dancing" to very loud *"alternative Christian music!"* Just the term "alternative" Should have been a dead giveaway to anyone with any discernment at all! There are NO *alternatives* to anything that is truly Christian. The well know "Christian artist" who was the featured performer, went on stage and yelled out "go crazy" to the audience before beginning to sing—and the crowd did just that! So much so that the key note speaker (who did discern what spiritual forces were at work) had to take authority over them by forbidding them to operate—in order to get the crowd under control.

49

One such recent advertisement I was sent for one of these kinds of gatherings said "prepare yourself for Holy Spirit encounter that you won't forget!" There are definitely "spiritual encounters" that are taking place, but I assure you they are not encounters with God's Holy Spirit.

Holiness and true reverence for many of the old hymns that were truly inspired by God's Spirit are being billed as "old wine" that is part of the old "religious order." God is being presented as a God that wants to see people "free" (not restrained in any way) to worship anyway that their emotions stirs them. What's even worse is that they think this flesh inspired soulish "radical worship" is a way of doing spiritual warfare! The truth is it is doing nothing more than manipulating and stirring up the emotions and imaginations of the masses, and even moving people into the realm of sorcery, such as those who sing and dance themselves into frenzied trances during pagan "worship" ceremonies. All this does is conjure up demonic spirits and gives them an entrance into the *forbidden realm of spirits*. Those leading these types of large gatherings engage in all kinds of extensive, long and drawn out, showy prayers that "come against" spiritual powers, which they call doing *spiritual warfare*. These prayers and "apostolic—prophetic warfare declarations" are usually coming from self-appointed, false apostles and prophets who lives are *not blameless* (either because of personal sins or because of false teaching) and they usually have their own agendas for doing what they do (i.e. money and finding followers).

How many souls do those who do this kind of spiritual warfare see come to true repentance and true salvation? I can tell you from years of being involved in these kinds of meetings that "salvation" from sin is not the focus. I do not recall ever seeing a call for repentance and salvation at any of these gatherings, nor was sin—repentance and salvation the topic of their teachings or sermons! The focus is on "building God's kingdom upon the earth NOW by getting entangled in the affairs of this life.

Jesus was clear about the fact that kingdom of God is not a physical kingdom to be built on earth by fighting against poverty, injustice or many other social causes. Neither is God's kingdom established by fighting for political, economic or religious power. Those who teach we need to take over the kingdoms of this world and establish governing rights over these things are not only teaching heresy, they are hindering people from entering into the "God's kingdom" which comes only through salvation from sin. Jesus said this to those who are doing this...

> *"How terrible it will be for you teachers... and you Pharisees. Hypocrites! For you won't let others enter the Kingdom of Heaven, and you won't go in yourselves... Yes, how terrible it will be for you teachers... and you Pharisees. For you cross land and sea to make one converts* (followers)*, and then you turn them into twice the sons of hell as you yourselves are. (Matthew 23:13-15, NLT, parenthesis mine).*

Again our confrontation with spiritual enemies means confronting their lies and doubts and combating these with the truth from God's word. We as spiritual warriors of God must take up our position as *kings* and *priests* within His Holy Nation and confront the lies of false teachings and the doubts they are producing in the minds of those who are hearing these false teachings...

> *Jesus Christ, the faithful witness, the firstborn from the dead, and the ruler over the kings of the earth. To Him who loved us and washed us from our sins in His own blood... and has made us kings and priests to His God and Father, to Him be glory and dominion* (not to us) *forever and ever (Revelation 1:5-6, NKJV, parenthesis mine).*

51

Please notice the prerequisite for becoming a king and priest, is to be... ***washed from our sins in His own blood***. We must be cleansed from ALL sin at ALL times in order to have God's delegated authority to war on His behalf by upholding His banner of truth. Just as the kings of God's Holy Nation in the Old Testament went to war against its enemies, we as Kings in the Holy Nation must confront the wiles of our enemies which have established strongholds within the minds of lost humanity. We do this by preaching the true Gospel of Christ and the whole, uncompromising truth of God's word. As priests we must minister cleansing and deliverance to those who respond to that word. However, if we are not "blameless" in our own entire being (spirit—soul—body) we will cringe under the accusations of the accuser and back away from confronting sin issues in the lives of others.

Satan especially targets those who stand in their "Joshua" priesthood. The word "Joshua" (Strong's 3091) means *Jehovah saves, or Jehovah delivers.* In our priestly ministry we are to be bringing salvation from sin and deliverance to those bound by the wiles of the devil. This again can only by accomplished by those who are cleansed and sanctified by God, and who have been given their garment of righteousness...

> *I will greatly rejoice in the LORD, My soul shall be joyful in my God; For He has clothed me with the garments of salvation, He has covered me with the robe of righteousness (Isaiah 61:10, NKJV).*

There are two people in the Old Testament who were called *Joshua.* One was Moses's successor (Deuteronomy 34:9-12), and a man who proved he was an exceptionally capable leader and military commander (Exodus 17:8-16). The other was Joshua the High Priest, who came out of exile from Babylon to restore the temple and its altar. Under him the priesthood was to be cleansed and purified (Zechariah 3:1-9). Many of God's true ministers are coming out of exile from *Babylon* (spiritual confusion) at this time and they are taking up their role as true priests in God's Holy Nation. The following text is one of my favorite passages of Scripture because it is a beautiful picture of how Jesus defends us as His "Joshua's" or priests who have been defiled by the false teachings of Babylon and are now looking to Him to make them Holy (for we cannot make ourselves holy or free ourselves from spiritual confusion and defilement)…

> *Then the angel showed me Joshua the high priest standing before the angel of the LORD* (Jesus)*. Satan was there at the angel's right hand, accusing Joshua of many things… And the LORD said to Satan, "I, the LORD, reject your accusations, Satan. <u>Yes, the LORD, who has chosen Jerusalem, rebukes you</u>. This man is like a burning stick that has been snatched from a fire." …Joshua's clothing was filthy as he stood there before the angel… So the angel said to the others standing there, "Take off his filthy clothes." And turning to Joshua he said, "See, <u>I have taken away your sins</u>, and now I am giving you these fine new clothes"(Zechariah 3:1-4, NLT).*

True warriors then are kings and priests who must be free from defiling sin issues in their lives; otherwise they will never be able to do true *spiritual warfare* by confronting the sin (error) in others. Sin issues makes us insecure, which means we will not obtain the objective previously mentioned, which is that of *"opening our mouths boldly"* in order to try and persuade sinners to repent and turn to Christ.

Insecurity issues find their root in the *fear of rejection*, which is the very reason people can't confront sin inside or outside of their church. False leaders shy away from sin issues because they fear being rejected by their followers, which means the loss of admiration—power and of course wealth. That is why these leaders have come up with so many unscriptural and "weird" ways of doing *spiritual warfare.* These things have become popular among insecure Christians because they don't have to confront sin and sinners! They can just *march—map* or *repent on behalf* of those who should be repenting for themselves. Any professing Christian, for that matter, who fears being rejected by those who need to be told truth concerning their sin, needs to examine themselves to see if they are really in the true faith, because Jesus promised His followers they would suffer rejection (or worse) if they chose to follow Him...

> *Examine yourselves as to whether you are in the faith. Test yourselves. Do you not know yourselves that Jesus Christ is* (really) *in you? — <u>unless indeed you are disqualified</u> (2 Corinthians 13:5, NKJV).*

If we are not willing to be seen as the scum of this earth, and suffer for righteousness sake, but prefer to believe that we have the authority and the ability to "war" away what we don't like... something is terribly wrong with our faith and Biblical view of what it means to be a true Christian warrior.

Biblical Principles For Warfare

Years ago while teaching on the subject of *spiritual warfare,* I was given a portion of Scripture by God concerning governing principles for warfare. I want to share a few things that I see regarding these principles. Following is the text that contains two of God's principles for warfare that I would like to expound upon...

> *"When you go out to battle against your enemies, <u>and see</u> horses and chariots and people more numerous than you, <u>do not be afraid of them</u>; for the LORD your*

54

> *God is with you, who brought you up from the land of Egypt... So it shall be, when you are on the verge of battle that the priest shall approach and speak to the people... And he shall say to them, 'Hear, O Israel: Today you are on the verge of battle with your enemies. Do not let your heart faint, do not be afraid, and do not tremble or be terrified because of them... for the LORD your God is He who goes with you, to fight for you against your enemies, to save you.' (Deuteronomy 20:1-4, NKJV).*

I would like to break this down into two very fundamental principles that will confirm what this study has been saying.

- **The first Principle** ...from the above text tells us: *Don't allow what you see with your natural senses to intimidate you.* It is overwhelming to see the sheer number of people in the world around us, that we need to share the Gospel with, who live their lives in a way that totally disrespects God and the Bible. Human nature feels comfortable doing or believing what "most" people seem to be also doing or believing. It makes them feel "normal." To be *normal* is how most people want to be perceived. However, we as true believers are not normal by the world's standard for normality and are in fact called God's *peculiar people.* We are called by God to share the message of the Gospel of Jesus Christ which requires we tell people that how they think and behave is not *normal* in God's eyes. In fact, we must tell them how they think and act is *wrong*! This will definitely not win us many popularity contests. Our message will without a doubt offend those who choose to believe there are no absolutes for right and wrong. What's more we must tell them the truth about their frightening eternal destination—if they are not willing to change their mind and ways and live according to God's standard for

55

normal. Our job is to do battle with the enemy by giving people the truth about their spiritual condition, without being intimidated by how they look in the natural. There will be a "butting of heads" with those who don't want to hear what God wants us to say...

> ***Speak to them with My words... will not listen to you and obey you since they will not listen to Me and obey Me, for all the house of Israel are impudent and stubborn of heart... Behold, I have made your face strong and hard against their faces and your forehead strong and hard against their foreheads... Like an adamant harder than flint or a diamond point have I made your forehead; fear them not, don't be dismayed at their looks (Ezekiel 3:4, 7-9, AMP).***

We cannot let how people respond affect us—while we battle for their very souls. Every true believer is called to *evangelize* the lost (give them the good news—after they understand the bad news that they are lost). This is not always easy but every good soldier must be willing to suffer hardship. This is what the ministry of genuine spiritual warfare is all about!

> ***As for you, be calm and cool and steady, accept and suffer unflinchingly every hardship, do the work of an evangelist, fully perform all the duties of your ministry (2 Timothy 4:5, AMP).***

In the text from (Deuteronomy 20:1-4) God's people are told not to be intimidated by the *horses* and *chariots* they would encounter during their battles. These typologies for these are worth investigating.

- **Horses** are powerful muscular animals (which are usually admired for their beauty and strength). Thus they represent dependence upon one's natural strength and they also represent one's self-reliance. These are qualities that our fallen human nature's most admire and even strive to achieve. As we seek to share the Gospel and persuade people to repent, we must not be intimidated by those beautiful looking people who come across as self-reliant and seem outwardly to have it all together. Sin makes all people insecure and fearful. Some people are just better at disguising this. Like the poor dirty looking street person, they too need to understand that they are poor, wretched sinners who need to repent and accept the salvation offered through Jesus Christ, or they will end up in the Lake of Fire.

- **Chariots** represent the *power and glory of human ingenuity* (cleverness and resourcefulness). We must not be intimidated by the intelligence and abilities attached to those *horses* (beautiful strong looking people who operate in the flesh). Otherwise we may refuse to enter the battle for their souls and we will not *boldly open our mouths and proclaim the truth*. We must never forget that it is not by our own abilities or strength that we go to war for their eternal destiny...

> *'Not by might nor by power, but by My Spirit,' Says the LORD of hosts (Zechariah 4:6, NKJV).*

The battle is the Lords ... God does not want us to be intimidated by the *chariots and horses* that we face in battle; but neither does He want those involved in spiritual warfare to trust in *horses* (their own strength) or in *chariots* (their intelligence and abilities) when it comes to battling *against principalities, powers and rulers*. He wants us totally dependent upon Him.

It has been stressed throughout this teaching, that we do not do battle with these spiritual enemies in the heavenlies, because our battle is with the *source* of what is influencing the minds of people here on earth (which comes from these spiritual enemies). The Lord Sabaoth is the Lord over the armies in the heavenlies. He alone deals with them! It is only by the power of God's presence through His Holy Spirit dwelling in us, that we will have the *strength* and *spiritual resources* (which include His spiritual gifts); to aggressively combat and cut off the sources of influences from these enemies...

> *Some trust in chariots, and some in horses: but we will remember the name of the LORD our God (Psalm 20:7 KJV).*
>
> *...for the LORD your God is He who goes* **with you,** *to fight for you against your enemies, to save you.' (Deuteronomy 20:4, NKJV).*

The Lord uses us here on earth to bring forth the messages He sends us forth with, while his warring angels fight in the heavenlies against the principalities, and rulers of darkness...

> *I have* **commanded** *My* **sanctified ones;** (His true saints) *I have also called My* **mighty ones** (brave warriors on earth and in heaven) *for My anger —* **Those who rejoice in My exaltation** (not their own) *...The noise of a multitude in the mountains, Like that of many people! A tumultuous noise of the kingdoms of nations gathered together!* **The LORD of hosts** (Sabaoath) **musters The army for battle...** *They come from a far country,* **From the end of heaven** *— The LORD*

58

SPIRITUAL WARFARE

*and **His   weapons*** (His   warriors)
of indignation (Isaiah 13:3-5, NKJV,
parenthesis mine).

In the above text the word **commanded** is the Hebrew
word (Strong's 6680) *tsavah* (tsaw-vaw') which means *to
appoint or send a messenger.* The word (Strong's 652)
apostle or apostolic in the New Testament also means
one who is sent. Therefore, God is showing us that in the
time of battle to destroy His enemies influence he uses
his armies (of sent ones) on earth—who are His apostolic
sanctified ones (holy ones), sent forth to give their
message of truth. While this is going on God says in
(vs. 4) he *musters His (heavenly) army from the far end
of heaven to fight in the battle!* Therefore we do our part
in God's army on earth and God's army in the heavenlies
does their part to accomplish what God intends. We must
leave the commanding of spiritual beings to the Lord and
get on with our mission of <u>boldly proclaiming the word
of truth.</u>

- **The second Principle for warfare** ...*deals with those
who are not ready to leave their civilian life behind.*
Those in this place will not be effective warriors. That is
also what the Apostle Paul told Timothy...

> *No one engaged in warfare **entangles
> himself with the affairs of this life**, that
> he may please him who enlisted him as a
> soldier (2 Tim 2:4, NKJV).*

In the text from (Deuteronomy 20:5-7), it mentions those
who fear the loss of *homes, businesses (i.e. vineyards)
and personal relationships,* because of becoming a
warrior. As we said earlier, when we fear confronting the
sin in our homes, on our jobs or in those we are have
intimate relationships with, it is because we fear the loss
these things. This means God's work is not our priority,
as it should be.

A true saint (holy—dedicated one), is called to be God's prophetic voice in all of these arenas. If (civilian things) are our priority, we are not qualified for the work of the ministry. We will be judged as to how we served in the service of our Lord...

> *So our aim is to please him always (who enlisted us in His army), whether we are here in this body or away from this body... For we must all stand before Christ to be judged. We will each receive whatever we deserve for the good or evil we have done in our bodies... We Are God's Ambassadors... It is because we know this solemn fear of the Lord that we work so hard to persuade others (2 Corinthians 5:9-11, NLT, parenthesis mine).*

In (Deuteronomy 20: 8) the issue of fear is addressed because fear is contagious. We cannot work and co-labor with those who are fearful. This means the work of the ministry is not for the fearful and fainthearted...

> *"The officers shall speak further to the people, and say, 'What man is there who is fearful and fainthearted? Let him go and return to his house, lest the heart of his brethren faint like his heart' (Deuteronomy 20:8, NKJV).*

We can clearly see then why it is so necessary to deal with our rejection, pride and bitterness issues. If we don't they will lead us into grave deception and ultimately be the cause of our spiritual death! I am sad to say that I cannot tell you the number of times I have seen this happen to Christians who refused to deal with these things. Our spiritual battle then is not for the dominion of governments, cultures or people. It is a battle for souls of men that are ruled by the fallen nature in mankind.

Everyone needs to know that Jesus Christ died so that they may have a new nature (His life) within them—which is a nature that loves God and hates sin. This is the only possible way that all things can be made new in their lives…

> *Therefore, if anyone is in Christ, he is a new creation; old things have passed away; behold, all things have become new (2 Corinthians 5:17, NKJV).*

Without men being transformed by the true Gospel of Christ, nothing ever changes. Why then have multitudes of professing Christians reverted to false methods of spiritual warfare, and laid down the real *work of the ministry,* which is that of bringing people eternal life through Christ. It is because those who are called to train and equip the followers of Jesus Christ, are drawing their attention away from the true *work of the ministry.* The focus is no longer on the fact that millions of people around the world each day are going through the gates of hell!

May the true seekers of God rise up and take up the ministry of their high calling and become ignited with a new passion to bring salvation through the preaching of repentance from sin and the Good News of Jesus Christ to all men in every nation!

> *Create in me a clean heart, O God, And*
> *renew a right spirit within me.*
> *Do not cast me away from Your presence,*
> *And do not take Your Holy Spirit from me.*
> *Restore to me the joy of Your salvation, And*
> *uphold me by Your generous Spirit.*
> *Then I will teach transgressors Your ways,*
> *And sinners shall be converted to You.*
> **(Ps 51:10-13, NKJV)**

By Karen E. Connell

IF POSSIBLE...Even the Very Elect Will Be Deceived

Many professing Christians are following ministers and ministries simply because they operate in signs and wonders. It is important to know what the Bible has to say about the subject of deception that Jesus said would be rampant in the end times in which we are living. Multitudes are falling prey to seducing spirits and doctrines of demons. In this book Karen is sounding the alarm with the hope that those who have ears will hear! (295 pages)

Investigating and Experiencing...The Glory of God

This booklet is an adapted from the *book IF POSSIBLE...Even the Very Elect Will Be Deceived*. This study is a biblical perspective on a most important but often misunderstood subject known as "The Glory of God." (68 pages)

NORMALIZING EVIL Through False Teaching

This book explores how the melding of various "Word of Faith" doctrines, such "prosperity teaching" and doctrines of the current *world transformation movement* are gaining momentum through a seducing spirit known as "Jezebel." Many Christians are not aware that they have been infected with deadly deceptions that have subtly invaded the body of Christ during the past few decades! It is time for professing Christians to start closely examining their beliefs in light of the Scriptures. Many are embracing teachings and teachers that misuse the Bible and who teach from Scriptures that are taken out of their context. We must take seriously the command to "rightly divide the word of God" so we will not fall prey to Satan's seducing spirits and doctrines of demons! (65 pages)

Content No Matter What!

Is it Possible to be content no matter what? We can choose to be BLESSED or STRESSED! This is the first in the *OVERCOMERS SERIES* of mini booklets. Karen Connell shares a Biblical perspective on many important issues so God's people can be overcomer's and not overcome by their life's circumstances.
(30 pages)

Spiritual Gifts Manual (213 pages)

Equipping the saints for the work of their ministry!

Enroll now in our FREE On Line or correspondence
Spiritual Gifts Course
This Spiritual Gifts Manual covers such subjects as:

• The different categories of gifts and their purpose

• How to identify the true operation and motivation for God's gifts.

• Identifying your spiritual gifts—and how to receive the gifts needed for your calling in the "work of your ministry"

All on-line students receive at no charge...

• The *Spiritual Gifts Manual* Through the mail or PDF on-line download

• Access to companion teachings by mp3 downloads or CD's by mail

• If preferred students can also take the course as a mail correspondence course

Upon finishing the course a *Certificate of Completion*
will be awarded to the student.

Three Fold Cord Healing and Deliverance Manual (225 pages)

Three Fold Cord Healing and Deliverance Manual & Teaching CD's

Professing Christians often struggle with things like anger, insecurity and worth issues simply because they lack healing and deliverance in all areas of their being, (body soul and spirit). The Biblical principle of the *three fold cord* states *"...a three fold cord is not easily broken" Eccl 4:12* This Manual and 24 CD companion teaching series, reveals how the three fold cord of *rejection—bitterness—pride* are the foundation for many physical, physiological and spiritual problems. Karen Connell shares key Biblical truths given to her by God during years of seeking His word for answers to her own struggles as a Christian; because of the physical, emotional and sexual abuse experienced in her own life. What Karen shares in this manual is the result of her *healing, deliverance* and *victory* over compulsive and addictive behavior, rooted in insecurity, anger and fear coming from the forces of darkness. Ministers and Christians in all walks of life have found victory through this material. You can too!

If you would like
Karen to speak at your
Church or group
You may contact her at…

extended_life@hotmail.com

Visit Our Website:

www.extendedlife.net

Please complete this form to place an order by mail... For more resources by Karen Connell go to: **www.extendedlife.net** resource page

Name_____

Address_____

City_____State_____Zip_____

Phone(   )_____e-mail_____

I have enclosed a love offering in the amount of $_____

- ▬ Please check if you would like to be placed on our mailing list

How many FREE copies of the following you would like?

___Copies of the *Extended Life C.T.M.* **Resource Catalog**

___Copies of the **Trumpet Sounds Volume #1 Booklet**

___Copies of: this months **Trumpet Sounds Newsletter**

___Copies of other resources listed below:

_____

_____

_____

_____

There is **no charge** for these products or for our newsletter; however any offering to help with production and mailing costs is always very much appreciated!
Checks may be made payable to:
Extended Life CTM
734 W. Water St. Hancock, MI 49930
Phone: (906) 482-6467